POEM SAFARI 2023

Party Animals

Edited By Briony Kearney

First published in Great Britain in 2023 by:
YoungWriters®
Est. 1991

Young Writers
Remus House
Coltsfoot Drive
Peterborough
PE2 9BF
Telephone: 01733 890066
Website: www.youngwriters.co.uk

All Rights Reserved
Book Design by Ashley Janson
© Copyright Contributors 2023
Softback ISBN 978-1-83565-005-9

Printed and bound in the UK by BookPrintingUK
Website: www.bookprintinguk.com
YB0MA0036F

FOREWORD

Dear Reader,

Welcome to this book packed full of feathery, furry and scaly friends!

Young Writers' Poetry Safari competition was specifically designed for 4-7 year-olds as a fun introduction to poetry and as a way to think about the world of animals. They could write about pets, exotic animals, dinosaurs or even make up their own crazy creature! From this starting point, the poems could be as simple or as elaborate as the writer wanted, using imagination and descriptive language.

Given the young age of the entrants, we have tried to include as many poems as possible. Here at Young Writers we believe that seeing their work in print will inspire a love of reading and writing and give these young poets the confidence to develop their skills in the future. Poetry is a wonderful way to introduce young children to the idea of rhyme and rhythm and helps learning and development of communication, language and literacy skills.

These young poets have used their creative writing abilities, sentence structure skills, thoughtful vocabulary and most importantly, their imaginations, to make their poems and the animals within them come alive. I hope you enjoy reading them as much as we have.

CONTENTS

Nettlesworth Primary School, Nettlesworth
Esme Thomson (5) — 1

New Oscott Primary School, Sutton Coldfield
Zaidan Azam (7) — 2
Theo Jones — 3

Northgate Primary School, Bishop's Stortford
Esmay Hampson (7) — 4
Safaa Dhila (7) — 5
Gabriel Bramall (6) — 6
Aarav Tiwari (7) — 7
Lena Adamska (7) — 8
Shay Blackett (7) — 9

Notre Dame Du Rosaire RC Primary School, St Peter Port
Maya Bailey (7) — 10

Our Lady & St Francis Primary School, Carfin
Sophia Brown (8) — 11

Panshanger Primary School, Welwyn Garden City
Sienna Lee-Lewis (6) — 12
Ema Matos (5) — 13

Park View Primary School, Prestwich
Zachary Shaw (6) — 14
Amanda Tarifi (6) — 15

Parkhill Primary School, Leven
Avijot Kaur (6) — 16

Pheasey Park Farm Primary School, Great Barr
Jayden Carville (7) — 17
Chloe Tete (6) — 18
Miah Matthews (7) — 19
Isabella Wallis (6) — 20

Pirton Hill Primary School, Luton
Lennon Miller (6) — 21
Jaskirat Cheema (6) — 22
Liyana Ahmed (6) — 23
Saif Almasoud (6) — 24

Polam Hall School, Darlington
Sukie Bonas (5) — 25
Harper Sung (6) — 26
Poppy Cunningham (6) — 27

Ratho Primary School, Ratho
Riley Brown (6) — 28

Robert Douglas Memorial School, Scone

Ebbie Bleakely (6)	29
Elliot Ryan Cargill (6)	30
Charlie Stirrat (7)	31
Jackson Fitzpatrick (6)	32
Archie Wilson (6)	33
Russell Coull (7)	34

Robsack Wood Primary Academy, St Leonards-On-Sea

Macey Taylor (6)	35
Archie Porterfield (7)	36
Rory Beattie (7)	37

S. Anselm's School, Bakewell

India Lacey (6)	38
Elsie Ward (5)	39
James Hainsworth (6)	40
Alexa Macintosh-Neal (6)	41
Vienna Oliver	42

Send CE Primary School, Send

Lilly O'Rourke (7)	43

Skelmorlie Primary School, Skelmorlie

Farrah Smith (6)	44

Smithy Bridge Primary School, Smithy Bridge

Zack Palmer (6)	45

St Andrew's Primary School, Burnfoot

Amellia McKendry (7)	46
Sophie Newbould (6)	47

St Anne's Catholic Primary School, Leyland

Naomi Tattersall (7)	48

St Bees Village Primary School, St Bees

Georgia Mahood (5)	49

St Bernadette's Catholic Primary School, Wombourne

Scarlet Bacon (7)	50
Ruby Bacon (5)	51
Alonso Jacholnik (6)	52

St Francis' Catholic Primary School, Goosnargh

Mickey Shorrock (5)	53
Oscar Kirwan (5)	54
Olivia Lockyer (4)	55
Ted Walling (4)	56

St John Paul II Primary School, Glasgow

Ayda Watt (7)	57
Jackson Hood (6)	58
Charis Chapo (8)	59
Haris Zafar (7)	60
Conall McMahon (7)	61
Sophia Brennan (7)	62
Evie-Rose McCourt (6)	63
Conell (6)	64
Kai Crombie (7)	65
Michael McCallion (7)	66

St John's CE Primary School, Keele

Luna Clift (7)	67
William Cohen (6)	68

St John's CE Primary School, Caterham

Jasmine Einecker (6)	69
Joshua Wooldridge (8)	70

St Joseph & St Teresa's Catholic Primary School, Woodlands

Dilan Karim (5)	71

St Joseph's Primary School, Antrim

Evelyn Suckling (6)	72

St Joseph's Primary School, Greenock

Aaron Reilly (7)	73
Rivers Robertson (7)	74
Aaron Relliy (7)	75

St Martin's CE (VA) Primary School, Scarborough

Jacob Blake (7)	76

St Mary's Catholic Primary School, Brierley Hill

Luca Sorano (7)	77

St Mary's Catholic Primary School, Newcastle-Under-Lyme

Charlie Jones (8)	78
Jackson Katabaazi (8)	79
Natasha Breese (8)	80

St Mary's CE Primary School, Tetbury

Marin Jackson (6)	81
Ivy Shepherd (6)	82

St Mary's Primary School, Bellanaleck

Alanna Corrigan (7)	83
Eloise Baxter (7)	84

St Mary's RC Primary School, Haddington

Georgie Thomson (7)	85
Ava Richardson (8)	86
Goda Skultinaite (8)	87
Lily MacArthur (7)	88
Danyl Morgan (8)	89
Melane Matuseva (7)	90
Emilija Lukjanova (7)	91
Claudia Stefaniak (7)	92

St Michael's CE Primary School, Sydenham

James Hearson (6)	93
Aaron Ndidi (7)	94
Amirah Costa (7)	95

St Oliver Plunkett Primary School, Belfast

Eva Donnelly (7)	96
Niall Angelone (7)	97
Aoife Hughes (7)	98

St Patrick's Primary School, New Stevenston

Connor Donnelly (6)	99
Caidan Hassan (6)	100
Ellie Cunningham (6)	101
Emillio Ferri (6)	102
Peter Sweeney (6)	103
Harris Doyle (7)	104

St Paul's CE Primary School, Chessington

Jonny Hammond (7)	105

St Richard's RC Primary School, Atherton

Oyinkan Ilupeju (7)	106

St Stephen's CE Primary School, Heath Town

Amarachi Ukaonu (6)	108

Stockham Primary School, Wantage

Tommy Harman (6)	109
Bobby Griffiths (6)	110

Thames View Primary School, Rainham

Mason Lanaway (6)	111
Leo Oldershaw (5)	112
Oscar Jarmak (6)	113

The Gateway Primary Academy, Dartford

Avanthika Aravinthan (5)	114
James Langdon (6)	115
Rachel Lin (5)	116

The Grove Academy, Garston

Vanesa Poloskinaite (7)	117

The Weatheralls Primary School, Soham

Urte Radaviciute (6)	118
Kieran Marsh (7)	119
Tallulah Rainbow Hanley Collings (6)	120

Kevin Rimkus (7)	121
Maja Spichalska (7)	122

Ton-Yr-Ywen Primary School, Cardiff

Harini Bejgum (6)	123

Tonyrefail Community School, Tonyrefail

Ralph Coombs (5)	124

Trawden Forest Primary School, Trawden

Jacob Smith (6)	125
Owen Grimes (6)	126

Tregadillett Primary School, Tregadillett

Toby Howard (7)	127

Tudor Grange Samworth Academy, Leicester

Egshiglen Giikhnaran (7)	128
Hadassah Festus (7)	129
Simrat Sohal (7)	130
Jessica Smart (8)	131
Chizzy Bilopez (7)	132
Misan Odogene (7)	133
Solace Akubue (7)	134
Esmae Hall (7)	135
Ronnie Chaplin (7)	136

Wendell Park Primary School, White City

Yagmur Susut (6)	137
Conor Naughton (5)	138

Westgate Primary School, Warwick

Samarjit Singh Ghotra (6)	139

Wickersley Northfield Primary School, Wickersley

Joshua Singleton (7)	140
George Lowe (7)	141
Elsie Jones (6)	142
Ethan Harris (7)	143

William Patten Primary School, London

Hafsa Kavalei (7)	144
Anna Violet Doxford (7)	145
E. Hirsch (7)	146
Ida de Courcy-Tollervey (8)	147
Ada Culha (6)	148
Nisa Caglar (7)	149

Willowbank Primary School, Cullompton

Omar Subhieh (5)	150

Winterton CE Infant School, Winterton

Florence McCague (5)	151

Woodlands Primary School, Borehamwood

Caoimhe Moran (6)	152

Woodville Primary School, Chelmsford

Inaaya Lawal (6)	153
Ollie Thomas (6)	154
Skyler-Rose Dudley (6)	155
Jenson Westgate (6)	156
Dusty Hall (6)	157

The Poems

Monkey

M onkeys are cheeky,
O r climb trees,
N ever feed him a sandwich,
K icking monkeys are
E verywhere,
Y ou must look out for them!

Esme Thomson (5)
Nettlesworth Primary School, Nettlesworth

What Am I?

I fight with other giraffes.
I am tall.
I am yellow and brown.
I have got short ears.
I am big.
I eat healthy leaves.
I have a black tail.
I have a black tongue.
What am I?

Answer: A giraffe.

Zaidan Azam (7)
New Oscott Primary School, Sutton Coldfield

What Am I?

I have two arms and two legs.
My face is small, cute and black.
My fur is brown and black.
I have a long tail to climb with.
What am I?

Answer: A spider monkey.

Theo Jones
New Oscott Primary School, Sutton Coldfield

Dolphin

D olphins are swimming in the dark sea
O val-shaped shells are clapping
L eaping dolphins are swimming
P arty dolphins are singing
H appy dolphins skipping
I n the sea, there are fish
N othing but kind and calm.

Esmay Hampson (7)
Northgate Primary School, Bishop's Stortford

Possums And Pythons

A diamanté poem

Python
Venomous, harmful
Slithering, gulping, eating
Fangs, scales, fur, tails
Hanging, playing dead, swimming
Fuzzy, stripy
Possums.

Aarav Tiwari (7)
Northgate Primary School, Bishop's Stortford

Lovely Anicorn

She can see the blue sunny sky
She can smell the yummy sweets
She eats rainbow soup with shiny sparkles
She feels the large, white clouds.

Lena Adamska (7)
Northgate Primary School, Bishop's Stortford

Armadillos And Toucans

Armadillo
Powerful, silly
Rolling, tumbling, sniffing
Perching, soaring, flapping
Lively, squawking
Toucan.

Shay Blackett (7)
Northgate Primary School, Bishop's Stortford

Snowflake

S oft, warm rabbit
N ever eats cooked vegetables
O n top of hay tucked up warm
W henever she's sad she cries
F unny when it jumps and hops
L ovely silky soft ears
A lways drinking water
K eeping healthy and strong
E verybody is scary to rabbits.

Maya Bailey (7)
Notre Dame Du Rosaire RC Primary School, St Peter Port

A German Shepherd

German shepherds look big and scary when you first meet,
But in the end, they all have five pads on their feet,
Their fur is black and tan and they're so cute,
I think sometimes I hear them play the flute.

Sophia Brown (8)
Our Lady & St Francis Primary School, Carfin

Parrot

P erches on trees.
A very fluffy body.
R ed, yellow and green
R are in Asia.
O nly found in rainforests.
T here are more than ten types of parrot.

Sienna Lee-Lewis (6)
Panshanger Primary School, Welwyn Garden City

The Cheeky Dog

I can smell dog food.
I can see amazing toys in a shop.
I can feel wet grass.
I can hear barking.
I can taste bones.

Ema Matos (5)
Panshanger Primary School, Welwyn Garden City

What Am I?

It is good.
It is nice.
I like it.
It climbs trees.
It runs fast.
It is scared of people.
It eats nuts.
What is it?

Answer: A squirrel.

Zachary Shaw (6)
Park View Primary School, Prestwich

The Cat

The cat is so fluffy,
She is as pretty as a flower,
And the cat is cuter than cute.

Amanda Tarifi (6)
Park View Primary School, Prestwich

Jolly Giraffe

S kinny, tall, long-necked giraffe, on the
A frican plain,
F loating amongst the tall leaves,
A ll the animals alert and aware,
R ed and brown patches
I n the golden sun.

Avijot Kaur (6)
Parkhill Primary School, Leven

Roary The Lion

Roary the lion who roared
Lions roared high in the sky
Someone came knocking on the door
The lion woke up and he was on the floor
The lion jumped out with an enormous roar
He roared like someone who snored
He wailed with a scare
Like someone who was scared
He had a long tail
And he had a letter in the mail
And he saw a snail.

Jayden Carville (7)
Pheasey Park Farm Primary School, Great Barr

A Giraffe Poem

G iraffes have tall, long necks.
I eat fresh, clean and yummy leaves.
R ain is a kind of water giraffes don't like.
A lso, they hide so they can stay warm.
F eed the giraffe leaves from the trees.
F eed the giraffe some water.
E at the leaves on the tree.

Chloe Tete (6)
Pheasey Park Farm Primary School, Great Barr

Elephant

E normous, big backs.
L ong, grey, skinny tail.
E lephants have big trunks.
P lay with little elephants.
H ow about you?
A nimals are playful.
N ow isn't that fantastic?
T he elephants are cute.

Miah Matthews (7)
Pheasey Park Farm Primary School, Great Barr

Lion

L ions galloping loudly.
I n the lion's cage, there is a lion.
O n the lion's tail, there are flies.
N ever go near a lion.

Isabella Wallis (6)
Pheasey Park Farm Primary School, Great Barr

What Am I?

I have four big feet
I have big ears
I have a black nose
I live in the sea
I have eyes like a dolphin
I have a blowhole
What am I?

Lennon Miller (6)
Pirton Hill Primary School, Luton

What Am I?

I have a fluffy nose
I am really cute
I have white fur
I love jumping
I don't bite
I am nice
What am I?

Jaskirat Cheema (6)
Pirton Hill Primary School, Luton

The Cutest Animal

It is white
It is fluffy
It is cute
It has blue and black eyes
It eats carrots
It hops and runs
What is it?

Liyana Ahmed (6)
Pirton Hill Primary School, Luton

What Am I?

I live somewhere cold
I eat fish
I am white
What am I?

Saif Almasoud (6)
Pirton Hill Primary School, Luton

My Favourite Pet

Once, there was a thief
And he was a chocolate-loving thief.
He once stole a cheetah,
And it was a spotty cheetah.
I loved the cheetah that he took,
As the cheetah that he took was my pet.

Sukie Bonas (5)
Polam Hall School, Darlington

This Is A Butterfly

I fly up into the sky.
Flapping my wings till I get up high.
Fluttering down,
I go and feast on nectar.

Harper Sung (6)
Polam Hall School, Darlington

Pandas

My animal is a panda.
Pandas eat bamboo,
And they are cute.
I love pandas.
Pandas run around.

Poppy Cunningham (6)
Polam Hall School, Darlington

The Honey Bear

Honey bears like to eat honey
Honey bears can smell the leaves
On the trees
Honey bears can see nature
Honey bears can feel the grass on
The ground
Honey bears can hear the wind blowing.

Riley Brown (6)
Ratho Primary School, Ratho

The Mouse

My mouse is cute
Like a teddy bear
Playful as a puppy
My mouse is as silly as a penguin falling over.

Ebbie Bleakely (6)
Robert Douglas Memorial School, Scone

The Snakes

It is as slimy as a snail
It is as scary as a spider
It is as dangerous as a ferocious tiger.

Elliot Ryan Cargill (6)
Robert Douglas Memorial School, Scone

Jaguar

It is as fast as a cheetah
It is as dangerous as a lion
It is fast as a big T-rex.

Charlie Stirrat (7)
Robert Douglas Memorial School, Scone

Snake

It is rough as a log
It is venomous like a black widow
It is scary like a spider.

Jackson Fitzpatrick (6)
Robert Douglas Memorial School, Scone

Dragon

It is as scary as a dinosaur
It can fly like an eagle
It eats meat like a brat.

Archie Wilson (6)
Robert Douglas Memorial School, Scone

The Monkey

It is as fluffy as a dog
It is as cute as teddy
It climbs as fast as a gorilla.

Russell Coull (7)
Robert Douglas Memorial School, Scone

Fox

It's a wild hunter,
Soft and cute
But not for stroking.
It's loving and really cute
But be careful
It can bite you.
If you see it at a zoo you might feed it.

Macey Taylor (6)
Robsack Wood Primary Academy, St Leonards-On-Sea

Sloth

Long arms,
Long legs,
Hangs on a tree a lot,
Sleeps on a tree a lot
And it is really fluffy.
It is as lazy as a lizard
And as sleepy as a cat.

Archie Porterfield (7)
Robsack Wood Primary Academy, St Leonards-On-Sea

Sea Fun

A salty, rushing wave,
Moving under like a dolphin,
Golden as the sun's rays,
Sparkly as a chest of treasure,
Smooth as a shiny pearl.

Rory Beattie (7)
Robsack Wood Primary Academy, St Leonards-On-Sea

What Am I?

I have fur that is orange
I have a wet nose
I am nocturnal
My nose is black
My fur is thick
I have black eyes
I eat chickens
What am I?

Answer: A fox.

India Lacey (6)
S. Anselm's School, Bakewell

What Am I?

I am as funny as a clown
I am as mean as a lion
I am as poisonous as a poisonous spider
What am I?

Answer: A clownfish.

Elsie Ward (5)
S. Anselm's School, Bakewell

What Am I?

I am deep and in the dark
I have little sparkles on my body
I am deadlier than an eel
What am I?

Answer: A viperfish.

James Hainsworth (6)
S. Anselm's School, Bakewell

What Am I?

I am as white as a cloud
I sing so softly
I am as big as a school
What am I?

Answer: A beluga whale.

Alexa Macintosh-Neal (6)
S. Anselm's School, Bakewell

What Am I?

I am as green as a pear
My fins are long
My head is as big as a rock
What am I?

Answer: A turtle.

Vienna Oliver
S. Anselm's School, Bakewell

Leopards

Leopards are big and bad,
The biggest cat I have ever had,
They crawl and scare at night,
This is where you hear them fight.

Lilly O'Rourke (7)
Send CE Primary School, Send

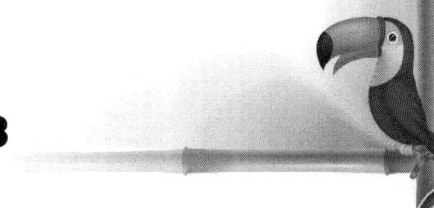

My Lhasa Apso

She is soft as a squishy teddy
She finishes her food in two seconds
She is protective
She sleeps in a jammy drawer.

Farrah Smith (6)
Skelmorlie Primary School, Skelmorlie

Dragons

A dragon can see the world
A dragon can smell his prey
A dragon can feel the ground
A dragon can hear the trees
A dragon can taste the air.

Zack Palmer (6)
Smithy Bridge Primary School, Smithy Bridge

My Giraffe

Giraffes have long necks as long as a pencil,
As big as a Christmas tree,
As furry as a puppy,
As smelly as a pig in mud,
As playful as a baby,
As regal as the Queen,
As big as a house,
As beautiful as a rose,
Walks like a sassy queen.

Amellia McKendry (7)
St Andrew's Primary School, Burnfoot

My Giraffe

As playful as a puppy,
As tall as a building,
As cuddly as a kitten,
As cute as a puppy.

Sophie Newbould (6)
St Andrew's Primary School, Burnfoot

Piggy

There are chubby pigs, skinny pigs and piggy pigs
They eat scraps of food
They are pink, light pink and dark pink.

Naomi Tattersall (7)
St Anne's Catholic Primary School, Leyland

George The Lion

George is a lion
George is kind
George like Ash.

Georgia Mahood (5)
St Bees Village Primary School, St Bees

Monkey

M onkeys like bananas so much!
O n a monkey's bottom, there is a curly tail.
N o one ever touches a monkey.
K eys are not good for monkeys because if they eat them, they will die.
E lla, the monkey, almost ate the key!
Y ou should never eat a monkey!

Scarlet Bacon (7)
St Bernadette's Catholic Primary School, Wombourne

Giraffe

G iraffes are tall.
I have seen a giraffe.
R eally long neck.
A giraffe likes to eat leaves.
F ragile and delicate.
F or leaves giraffes like to smell and eat.
E legant giraffes.

Ruby Bacon (5)
St Bernadette's Catholic Primary School, Wombourne

Cheetah

C heetahs are fast.
H airy.
E lement of a cheetah is fast.
E pic cheetahs.
T he cheetahs are fast like racing cars.
A re they smooth?
H unt for food!

Alonso Jacholnik (6)
St Bernadette's Catholic Primary School, Wombourne

My Tiger

My tiger roars.
My tiger eats parrots.
My tiger is rough.
My tiger likes to eat.
My tiger looks scary.

Mickey Shorrock (5)
St Francis' Catholic Primary School, Goosnargh

Snappy Snaps

Snappy was in his garden.
Snappy was making mud pie.
When Mummy called him in,
Snappy snapped!

Oscar Kirwan (5)
St Francis' Catholic Primary School, Goosnargh

Olivia Unicorn

Olivia Unicorn is sweet,
Olivia Unicorn is kind,
Olivia Unicorn is soft and happy.

Olivia Lockyer (4)
St Francis' Catholic Primary School, Goosnargh

My Dog, Bolt

My dog smells lovely.
My dog barks.
My dog feels soft.
My dog eats bones.

Ted Walling (4)
St Francis' Catholic Primary School, Goosnargh

Parrot

P arrots are fluffy, red, blue, white and yellow
A nd they live in a jungle, rainforest and zoo
R eally fast
R eally funny
O n summer days they fly a lot
T hey sometimes live in trees too.

Ayda Watt (7)
St John Paul II Primary School, Glasgow

Tigers

T he tiger is extremely terrifying
I ntelligently sneaky when it's looking for food
G ingery fur
E xcellent at catching prey
R eally, really furry.

Jackson Hood (6)
St John Paul II Primary School, Glasgow

Whales

W hales are cute
H owever, they sometimes spray water at you
A t the ocean you can see them sometimes
L oves to swim
E very day they eat fish.

Charis Chapo (8)
St John Paul II Primary School, Glasgow

Puppies

P uppies are cute
U p and down they jump
P uppies are black and white
P uppies can be fun
Y orkshire is a type of dog.

Haris Zafar (7)
St John Paul II Primary School, Glasgow

Monkey

M ad monkey
O n a tree
N aughty
K id
E ats bananas
Y ells and swings.

Conall McMahon (7)
St John Paul II Primary School, Glasgow

Monkey

M ad monkey
O utside
N ice
K ind
E ats bananas
Y ellow bananas.

Sophia Brennan (7)
St John Paul II Primary School, Glasgow

Chick

C hubby
H airy
I t eats seeds
C ute
K ids like them.

Evie-Rose McCourt (6)
St John Paul II Primary School, Glasgow

The Desert House

C lever
A nimal
M uscular
E yelashes
L oyal.

Conell (6)
St John Paul II Primary School, Glasgow

Cats

C ats eat cat food
A nd then miaow
T he cats are fluffy.

Kai Crombie (7)
St John Paul II Primary School, Glasgow

Dogs

D igs holes
O n its dog bed
G ood as gold.

Michael McCallion (7)
St John Paul II Primary School, Glasgow

What Am I?

A kennings poem

High flyer,
Sharp scratcher,
Mighty drifter,
Tree sleeper,
Eagle lover,
Snake eater,
Clever grabber,
What am I?

Luna Clift (7)
St John's CE Primary School, Keele

What Am I?

They have white fur,
They have soft fur,
They have cuddly fur,
They have four legs,
It's a sheep!

William Cohen (6)
St John's CE Primary School, Keele

Monkeys

M onkeys climb tall trees
O n their bodies, they have big ears
N ice bananas
K now that monkeys like bananas
E ats loudly
Y awn quietly.

Jasmine Einecker (6)
St John's CE Primary School, Caterham

The Lion

The lion loves eating meat
He lives in a cave
He comes at night
He has lots of teeth and they are sharp!
He has big ears to hear from.

Joshua Wooldridge (8)
St John's CE Primary School, Caterham

Fish

F antastic curls
I mportant swimmer
S uper shiny scales
H appy to sparkle.

Dilan Karim (5)
St Joseph & St Teresa's Catholic Primary School, Woodlands

On Safari

Leopards are fast.
Hyenas laugh.
Lions hunt.
Giraffes have long necks.
Hippos are stinky.

Evelyn Suckling (6)
St Joseph's Primary School, Antrim

The Christmasaurus

He smells like a cold fresh drink on a hot day
He looks like a friendly blue flower covered in frost
He sounds like roar, roar, roar
He feels like icy snow
He tastes like a fresh minty candy cane
He is the Christmasaurus.

Aaron Reilly (7)
St Joseph's Primary School, Greenock

My Dog Poem

Dogs smell like mud and are stinky
Dogs look fluffy and kind
Dogs sound like bark, bark, bark
Dogs feel cosy and cuddly
Dogs taste like sausage and bacon
I love dogs!

Rivers Robertson (7)
St Joseph's Primary School, Greenock

My Sub Creature Poem

Subs smell like nothing
Subs look like red rock
Subs sound like subscribe
Subs feel fluffy
Subs taste like delicious sweets.

Aaron Relliy (7)
St Joseph's Primary School, Greenock

Rhino

A kennings poem

A horn fighter.
A good sleeper.
A friend flipper.
An amazing fighter.
A slow walker.
A good listener.

Jacob Blake (7)
St Martin's CE (VA) Primary School, Scarborough

What Am I?

It is long.
It has hard skin.
It has a very red tongue.
It is yellow.
What is it?

Answer: It is a snake.

Luca Sorano (7)
St Mary's Catholic Primary School, Brierley Hill

Timmy The Tiger's Poem

Tigers smell like meat,
Like they always eat,
Tigers look like wild cats
That hunt every day and night,
Tigers sound like lions
When they roar,
Tigers feel fluffy,
Just like my dog,
Tigers are very protective,
And they are very rough,
Tigers can see animals
That are trying to sneak up on them.

Charlie Jones (8)
St Mary's Catholic Primary School, Newcastle-Under-Lyme

The Manticore

The manticore smells like fresh mint,
The stench they make makes my eyes squint,
They sound like lions, they feel furry,
And never blurry,
Manticores taste like toothpaste,
And they look like cats and scorpions,
And they like toothpaste, which is their toothpaste.

Jackson Katabaazi (8)
St Mary's Catholic Primary School, Newcastle-Under-Lyme

My Giraffe Poem

Gerry the giraffe smells of grass,
And is all smelly and stinky,
Giraffes are soft and fluffy,
Like your bed,
Giraffes look lazy and very dozy,
Giraffes are fierce,
Giraffes taste like meat with hair on,
That's my giraffe.

Natasha Breese (8)
St Mary's Catholic Primary School, Newcastle-Under-Lyme

What Am I?

I am a mammal
My fur is black and white
I live in China
I am a herbivore
I eat bamboo
I am very slow
What am I?

Answer: A panda.

Marin Jackson (6)
St Mary's CE Primary School, Tetbury

What Am I?

I have a spiky tail
I have sharp teeth
I am a carnivore
What am I?

Answer: A crocodile.

Ivy Shepherd (6)
St Mary's CE Primary School, Tetbury

Robins In The Winter

Robins, robins, they are so cute
They sing us songs and we give them food.
Robins, robins, they jump so fast
And they remind us of people from the past.
Robins, robins, they make me smile
And I like to watch them for a while.
Robins, robins, in the snow
They leave wee footprints wherever they go.

Alanna Corrigan (7)
St Mary's Primary School, Bellanaleck

Koalas

Koalas, koalas, you are fluffy
You make me laugh
You like eating leaves
And live in trees
And you hang from trees.

Eloise Baxter (7)
St Mary's Primary School, Bellanaleck

My Magical Animal

Soars through the sky,
Terrific at climbing,
Rubies are its favourite thing,
It loves singing,
Perfect as a pet,
Everyone adores it,
You'd love it too,
Prettier than a poodle,
One has a baby pegasus,
Loveable for all,
Available for all to see,
Ruffles on their whiskers,
Beauty everywhere they go,
Everyone is welcome to see its lovely show,
And when it needs excitement, it rains glitter everywhere.

Georgie Thomson (7)
St Mary's RC Primary School, Haddington

The Amazing Polly

P olly the parrot soars like an eagle,
A chatterbox she is,
R eally good at jokes and is fun,
R ainbow colours rush through her feathers,
O h, she's so amazing,
T ake a cuddle, she's so cute.

Ava Richardson (8)
St Mary's RC Primary School, Haddington

Butterfly

B eautiful patterns,
U sing wings to fly,
T iny,
T eenie,
E xcited,
R eally likes her friend,
F lying,
L oving,
Y ummy butter to eat.

Goda Skultinaite (8)
St Mary's RC Primary School, Haddington

Giraffe

G iraffes are tall,
I t eats grass,
R uns really fast,
A tall animal,
F airies can't even reach,
F ew people are taller than them,
E ats off trees.

Lily MacArthur (7)
St Mary's RC Primary School, Haddington

Dolphin

D olphins eat sharks,
O n the open waters,
L oving dolphins,
P ets are dolphins,
H uggers,
I n the air, dolphins are leaping,
N ight hunters.

Danyl Morgan (8)
St Mary's RC Primary School, Haddington

Kitten

K ittens like jumping,
I s a cat crazy?
T he cat likes tins,
T he cat is crazy!
E very cat likes eating fish,
N ice kittens like playing.

Melane Matuseva (7)
St Mary's RC Primary School, Haddington

Kitten

K ittens are cute,
I n the home where they live,
T hey like to play,
T hey like to play,
E at fish,
N aughty but fluffy.

Emilija Lukjanova (7)
St Mary's RC Primary School, Haddington

Sheep

S heep are fun and they are
H appy and cute, and they
E at grass,
E very sheep is fluffy,
P eople like sheep.

Claudia Stefaniak (7)
St Mary's RC Primary School, Haddington

The Meerkat In Egypt

It looks like a prairie dog.
It eats long, thin grass and yellow, blue and orange scorpions.
It has big, wide eyes that stare at you.
It lives in a burrow under the ground to stay safe.
It's friendly and fluffy.
It smells like hot sand.
It's a meerkat from Egypt!

James Hearson (6)
St Michael's CE Primary School, Sydenham

What Am I?

It has scaly, red skin.
It breathes hot, dangerous fire.
It's mean and fast.
It has strong, heavy wings.
It can fly through the clouds.
It's a dragon!

Aaron Ndidi (7)
St Michael's CE Primary School, Sydenham

The Mystery Animal

I can change colour.
I have a long, scaly tail.
I can climb trees.
I only eat plants and bugs.
I live in the rainforest.
I am a lizard!

Amirah Costa (7)
St Michael's CE Primary School, Sydenham

Tigers

T igers hunt for food,
I n the jungle, tigers run very fast,
G rr! I hope I don't meet a tiger,
E very tiger has a thin tail and stripes on their bodies,
R un as fast as a speeding car.

Eva Donnelly (7)
St Oliver Plunkett Primary School, Belfast

Snaking Around

S neaks around looking for prey,
N ever lives in a desert,
A re devious and cold-blooded creatures,
K ills other reptiles with their sharp fangs,
E ats amphibious creatures.

Niall Angelone (7)
St Oliver Plunkett Primary School, Belfast

All About Turtles

T urtles have a hard shell,
U nderwater, they swim,
R unning fast to the water,
T urtles like making friends,
L ive underwater,
E at seagrass and algae.

Aoife Hughes (7)
St Oliver Plunkett Primary School, Belfast

Bunny

B unnies always steal my carrots.
U nder the ground at the zoo Bunny lives.
"**N** o more carrots for you," said the man at the zoo.
N o more carrots left, so he got some from the shop.
"**Y** ou are so cute," said the man to the bunny.

Connor Donnelly (6)
St Patrick's Primary School, New Stevenston

Monkey

M onkeys eat bananas in the trees.
O n trees, they throw banana splits.
N ever ever steal monkeys' bananas.
K icking the trees and playing on the swings.
E very day they play tag in the jungle.
Y esterday they played banana ball.

Caidan Hassan (6)
St Patrick's Primary School, New Stevenston

Bunny

B unnies dig holes under muck.
U nder a hole there is a white bunny.
N ice bunnies are drinking milkshakes on a holiday.
N aughty bunnies are singing on a holiday.
"**Y** ou are a great bunny," said the girl.

Ellie Cunningham (6)
St Patrick's Primary School, New Stevenston

Cobra

C obras rock because they have venom.
O n their bodies, they have hundreds of green scales.
B e careful if you see one.
R un if you startle one.
A cobra is a dangerous creature!

Emillio Ferri (6)
St Patrick's Primary School, New Stevenston

Gecko

G eckos grab food with their tongues.
E very gecko eats insects.
C an they grab stuff with their tail?
K ind geckos like people.
O n trees, they like to play.

Peter Sweeney (6)
St Patrick's Primary School, New Stevenston

T-Rex

T -rexes stomp about a lot.
R oaring wherever they go.
E arthquakes every day and night.
X -ray a T-rex if it hurts its foot.

Harris Doyle (7)
St Patrick's Primary School, New Stevenston

Mammoth

M ammoths are so strong and buff that
A mammoth can break a wall
M ammoths are so cool
M agnificent tusks on their face
O h my gosh, he's so fluffy
T he fur on his body is to keep him warm
H e is so loud like me!

Jonny Hammond (7)
St Paul's CE Primary School, Chessington

The Lost Butterfly

I have a butterfly who doesn't know what she is,
Every time I look into her eyes, I feel surprised,
She never smiles or cries, I think and think again,

Her wings are majestic, one of a kind,
I look at other butterflies, none like her I find,
She has a secret talent,
That she never shows,

Promise me you won't tell anyone, even people you know,
Can you hear me speak? Loud and clear,
When she moves her wings, the colours pop in the beautiful glow,
When her face goes gloomy, the weather gets a bit moody,

My butterfly is so special, but most special to me,
To others, she's like any other butterfly; to me, she's my amazing wonder.
Just for me.

Oyinkan Ilupeju (7)
St Richard's RC Primary School, Atherton

Snake

The snake's teeth are as sharp as a sword.
The snake's skin is as clean as clean hands and shiny marble.
The snake's new skin is as colourful as sweets.
The snake's eyes are as tiny as a tiny, tiny dot.
The snake is dangerous.
The snake is as long as a rope.
The snake is as slow as a slug.
The snake is as sneaky as a tiger.

Amarachi Ukaonu (6)
St Stephen's CE Primary School, Heath Town

My Dog Poem

My dog can see trees,
My dog smells like a sausage,
My dog is small and fluffy,
My dog can hear me.

Tommy Harman (6)
Stockham Primary School, Wantage

My Dog Poem

My dog is cute,
My dog rolls in the mud,
My dog is cute.

Bobby Griffiths (6)
Stockham Primary School, Wantage

What Am I?

I live in the snow.
I lay eggs.
I have a yellow chest.
I am black and white.
I like to eat fish.
I like to slide on my belly.
What am I?

Answer: A penguin.

Mason Lanaway (6)
Thames View Primary School, Rainham

What Am I?

I have a sharp fin.
I eat fish.
I live in the water.
What am I?

Answer: A shark.

Leo Oldershaw (5)
Thames View Primary School, Rainham

What Am I?

I say *neigh!*
I eat hay.
I live in a field.
What am I?

Answer: A horse.

Oscar Jarmak (6)
Thames View Primary School, Rainham

My Cat

My cat is black and white and on my finger it bites.
She loves chicken and fish in her blue cat dish.
My cat has white sharp claws and born short paws.
My cat has a stripy long tail and in the game she fails.
It has whiskers and rips the gold large stickers.
My cat climbs on a tree and the leaves are green.
My cat runs around and loves being found.
She sits on the mat and she's very fat.
It kicks the ball and the ball hits the wall.

Avanthika Aravinthan (5)
The Gateway Primary Academy, Dartford

Snakes

An anaconda is a sneaky snake
I met one once, a big mistake!
They are terrifying, they make me scared
So if you see one be prepared
They like to eat fish in their tummies
And rodents too are very yummy.

James Langdon (6)
The Gateway Primary Academy, Dartford

Fly In The Air

Come out at night.
Fly searching for yummy food.
Sleeping upside down on the trees.
Don't wake them up.
Little bats with big families.
It's too crowded but warm.

Rachel Lin (5)
The Gateway Primary Academy, Dartford

What Is It?

It is as fluffy as a teddy bear
It is as cute as a panda
It is as little as an ant
Its magic is as colourful as a rainbow
It has a horn that is gold
What is it?

Answer: A unicorn.

Vanesa Poloskinaite (7)
The Grove Academy, Garston

A Cat

I am a cat.
I go through the shimmering, little tunnel to get into my home.
I can see a black and marshmallow-white road to walk on.
I can smell some nice, delicious, good food to eat in my home.
I can hear someone sad, kind and muscly, so I go to help him.
I can feel a soft, fluffy, huge mat.
I can taste new, delicious food all for me in my beautiful home because my owner gave me my dinner so I wasn't hungry anymore.

Urte Radaviciute (6)
The Weatheralls Primary School, Soham

A Puppy

I am a puppy and...
I can see another pretty dog.
I can hear the doorbell ringing.
I can feel the green, wavy grass.
I can taste lovely, yummy, crunchy carrots.
I can smell beautiful food cooking.

Kieran Marsh (7)
The Weatheralls Primary School, Soham

The Happy Dolphin

I am a dolphin,
I have grey fins and eyes,
I am beautiful and pretty,
I go up to the surface to breathe,
Because dolphins can't stay underwater,
Anyway, it is nice to be a dolphin!

Tallulah Rainbow Hanley Collings (6)
The Weatheralls Primary School, Soham

What Am I?

I can see yummy, tasty food.
I can hear squeaky, playful mice.
I can taste delicious, wet fish.
I can feel the soft, comfy sofa.
I can smell the tall, green grass.
I am a cat.

Kevin Rimkus (7)
The Weatheralls Primary School, Soham

A Cat

I am a cat and...
I can see the rain outside.
I can hear the leaves falling.
I can smell the milk.
I can taste my cat food.
I can feel the mice.
I am a fluffy cat.

Maja Spichalska (7)
The Weatheralls Primary School, Soham

I Have A Pet Bunny

I have a pet
She lives in a hutch
She nibbles carrots
She eats so much
With long brown ears
And a twitching nose
In and out
Of her hutch she goes.

Harini Bejgum (6)
Ton-Yr-Ywen Primary School, Cardiff

Run Fast Like A Cheetah

T eeth sharp
I t prowls
G ets meat to eat
E yes glow in the dark
R un fast like a cheetah.

Ralph Coombs (5)
Tonyrefail Community School, Tonyrefail

Grizzly Bears

Grizzly bears feel soft and itchy like my woolly hat,
Grizzly bears taste like chocolate buttons,
Grizzly bears smell like stinky socks and wet dogs,
Grizzly bears sound like *roar, growl!*
Grizzly bears look brown and terrifying.

Jacob Smith (6)
Trawden Forest Primary School, Trawden

Tigers

Tigers smell like a rotten tree,
Tigers look like a stripy teddy bear,
Tigers feel soft and fluffy,
Tigers taste hot and spicy as a chilli pepper,
It sounds like a dragon.

Owen Grimes (6)
Trawden Forest Primary School, Trawden

Crazy Axolotl

My name is Axolotl and I come from Mexico,
If I lose an arm or leg don't worry, it will regrow.
I live underwater but also have lungs,
My cousin, the salamander, wishes he was just as cool as me.

Toby Howard (7)
Tregadillett Primary School, Tregadillett

What Am I?

My body is black and white like a zebra
But unlike a zebra, I only have two legs.
I have giant wings but I can't fly.
I like to eat snakes or ants and sometimes even leaves.
I like to dash in deserts and scurry in the sand.
My mouth can be mistaken for two pointy knives when scooping fish from the sea.
You may think I'm a penguin because I lay my own eggs but I sprint instead of waddling.

Answer: I am an ostrich.

Egshiglen Giikhnaran (7)
Tudor Grange Samworth Academy, Leicester

What Am I?

I have soft, fluffy fur but I'm not a dog.
I'm cute and small but not tiny.
Lazy is my middle name.
I like to sit and watch the world go by.
My favourite toy is a cotton wool ball.
Touch me and I will scratch.
I can drink cold milk all day long.
Put me in the sun and watch me sleep.
My four little legs help me run as fast as Sonic.
What am I?

Answer: I am a cat.

Hadassah Festus (7)
Tudor Grange Samworth Academy, Leicester

What Am I?

I am as heavy as a giant rock.
My body is the colour of an orange.
I have white, sharp teeth which can break anything.
When I growl you will hide!
I am as fierce as a lion.
If I run I sound like a zooming rocket.
Stay away from me, I am a carnivore.
Watch me pounce for food.
You should be happy I don't live near you.
What am I?

Answer: I am a tiger.

Simrat Sohal (7)
Tudor Grange Samworth Academy, Leicester

What Am I?

I'm huge and friendly but don't touch me because I'll nibble you up.
I'll eat plants or leaves, maybe even some carrots.
My tongue is black from wandering around in the sun for far too long.
You might think I'm a cheetah for my spots but I'm not.
I'm the tallest living land animal around.
What am I?

Answer: I am a giraffe.

Jessica Smart (8)
Tudor Grange Samworth Academy, Leicester

What Am I?

I have a fluffy body and a cute face.
My size is as small as a mouse.
You have never seen anything as friendly as me.
I run as fast as a cheetah.
My special skill is escaping.
You are safe, I'm a herbivore!
Don't shout or I'll crouch in the corner.
I can fit in your hand.
What am I?

Answer: I am a hamster.

Chizzy Bilopez (7)
Tudor Grange Samworth Academy, Leicester

What Am I?

I have sharp claws like a knife
But don't hold me or I will eat you up.
I'm mostly asleep all day
But interrupt me and I will kill you.
I'm very protective of my cubs
But come close to them and I will chase you away.
I belong to the cat family
But I'm not as purry as you think.

Answer: I am a lion.

Misan Odogene (7)
Tudor Grange Samworth Academy, Leicester

What Am I?

I can run as fast as a lion but I have teeth like a horse.
I have stripes like a tiger but not as colourful.
I use my strong teeth to graze on grass.
My hooves stride along the desert under the hot sun as I look for shade.
My tongue is as black as night and bendy as a rubber band.

Answer: I am a zebra.

Solace Akubue (7)
Tudor Grange Samworth Academy, Leicester

What Am I?

I am a big animal.
I like to swing in trees.
I like to eat bananas.
I like to make sounds like, "*Oo!*" and, "*Aa!*"

Answer: I am a monkey.

Esmae Hall (7)
Tudor Grange Samworth Academy, Leicester

What Am I?

I am a big animal.
I like to eat bananas.
I like to swing in the trees.
I make sounds like, "*Oo!*" and, "*Aa!*"

Answer: I am a monkey.

Ronnie Chaplin (7)
Tudor Grange Samworth Academy, Leicester

The Big Cat

A cheetah is an animal
Marvellous and royal.

My big cat is fluffy,
It runs very speedily.

That cheetah is fierce,
It can give you tears.

It is black and yellow,
It lives where the sun is mellow.

Yagmur Susut (6)
Wendell Park Primary School, White City

Pandas

P andas eat bamboo
A nd sleep in the
N ight
D o they like pencils?
A nd do they like other pandas?

Conor Naughton (5)
Wendell Park Primary School, White City

Safari

In the morning, at 8:30,
We went on the bus and went to Safari.
I put my lunchbox in my bag.
I had lots of fun
Then we went home.

Samarjit Singh Ghotra (6)
Westgate Primary School, Warwick

Frog

My frog is as cheeky as a monkey
He is a front-flipping frog
He does it every day
He gets hurt... *Bang! Bang! Bang!*
This frog is as happy as a smiley face
It is as stinky as slime
The frog is as bald as Haaland
The fancy posh frog
The frog loves eating flies.

Joshua Singleton (7)
Wickersley Northfield Primary School, Wickersley

Terrifying Lion

Fur that is black and blue
Eyes glitter in the night
Fast like a Ferrari
And sneaky like a detective
Tail like a gold Lamborghini
You can't see it in the sun
With terrifying teeth
And ear-splitting roar
Watch out for the terrifying lion.

George Lowe (7)
Wickersley Northfield Primary School, Wickersley

Furry Fox

Fur as red as a ladybug
Nose as black as coal
Fluffy, friendly, furry fox
Eyes as sparkly as diamonds
Wonderful wild fox
As red as a rocket flame
Fantastic fox
Friendly fox
Fluffy fox
Pointy ears
Wild fox
Twitchy nose.

Elsie Jones (6)
Wickersley Northfield Primary School, Wickersley

Terrifying Tiger!

It roars like a terrified person
The fur is like a bunny
Teeth as sharp as a knife
The claws are like a sword
Runs like a Ferrari
The eyes are glowing green.

Ethan Harris (7)
Wickersley Northfield Primary School, Wickersley

My Cat

My cat, with super sensitive
Nose, smells treats!
He can always taste food.
Prince is like a soft, cuddly toy
Prince can always feel a soft blanket.
He thinks he is a beast
When he has a feast!
When he is curious,
He might get furious.
He can feel the wind
Because he is normally outside.
When he walks on moss
He thinks he is the boss!

Hafsa Kavalei (7)
William Patten Primary School, London

The Fierce Tiger!

The fierce tiger eats marvellous meat before he
Sleeps.

The fierce tiger is soft and stripy but
If you touch him, then he will go rough.

The fierce tiger smells meat from miles
And then he smiles.

The fierce tiger can hear from a long way away
From the bay.

The fierce tiger can see from quite far
And he can see the spa.

Anna Violet Doxford (7)
William Patten Primary School, London

The Powerful Sabretooth Tiger

The powerful sabretooth tiger
Gobbles up people all day long.

It can hear from miles and miles

He's so hairy, you can smell him
For miles and miles

He's so soft, but if you touch him
He will bite you

His eyes are made out of
Lasers and he could laser
You.

E. Hirsch (7)
William Patten Primary School, London

The Lazy Liger

The lazy liger's large paws
Affects the lazy liger's large roars.
Whilst swallowing meat
It's hard to greet
Animals that you'd rather eat.
The lazy liger is as jumpy as a frog.
Ruby-red eyes
Glimmering in the night skies.

Ida de Courcy-Tollervey (8)
William Patten Primary School, London

The Cheeky Chimpanzee

The cheeky chimpanzee
Smiles at me
The cheeky chimpanzee
Winks at me
The cheeky chimpanzee
Smells like
Bananas.

Ada Culha (6)
William Patten Primary School, London

The Fastest Cheetah In The World

A cheetah can eat.
A cheetah can run.
A cheetah can hear.
A cheetah can smell.
A good cheetah can hunt good.

Nisa Caglar (7)
William Patten Primary School, London

Who Am I?

She is as long as a tree.
She is as cheeky as a rabbit.
She is as sneaky as a wolf.
She is as greedy as a tiger.
She is as black as night.
She is as slow as a worm.
Do you know what I am?

Answer: It is a snake!

Omar Subhieh (5)
Willowbank Primary School, Cullompton

The Fluffy Sheep

Cute and pretty,
Fluffy and nice,
Friendly and pretty,
Soft and shiny.

Florence McCague (5)
Winterton CE Infant School, Winterton

Trixie

Trixie looks stripy, spotty, soft and smooth
Because I brush her every week
Trixie sounds crazy and loud
Because she goes *neigh!*
My horse smells like minty fresh flowers
Because she has a big flower field
Trixie feels hot, dry and rough
When it's a hot, summery day.

Caoimhe Moran (6)
Woodlands Primary School, Borehamwood

Cheetah

C heetahs hunt for animals
H ide in camouflage
E xtra, extra fast!
E ats raw animals!
T oo fast for you!
A nimals better hide
H ot countries.

Inaaya Lawal (6)
Woodville Primary School, Chelmsford

Octopus

O ctopus has eight legs
C urls around rocks
T entacles waving
O n water
P ink, orange, grey
U nderwater
S wimming.

Ollie Thomas (6)
Woodville Primary School, Chelmsford

Kitten

K ills mice
I t likes to sleep
T igers are a little bit like a cat
T wice it sleeps
E xcellent pet
N ibbles on toys.

Skyler-Rose Dudley (6)
Woodville Primary School, Chelmsford

Wolf

W olf Jenson
O ver in the woods
L oves to eat meat
F ierce and powerful.

Jenson Westgate (6)
Woodville Primary School, Chelmsford

Tiger

T errifying
I t is beautiful
G rowls
E ats meat
R oars!

Dusty Hall (6)
Woodville Primary School, Chelmsford

YOUNG WRITERS INFORMATION

We hope you have enjoyed reading this book – and that you will continue to in the coming years.

If you're the parent or family member of an enthusiastic poet or story writer, do visit our website **www.youngwriters.co.uk/subscribe** and sign up to receive news, competitions, writing challenges and tips, activities and much, much more! There's lots to keep budding writers motivated!

If you would like to order further copies of this book, or any of our other titles, then please give us a call or order via your online account.

Young Writers
Remus House
Coltsfoot Drive
Peterborough
PE2 9BF
(01733) 890066
info@youngwriters.co.uk

Join in the conversation!
Tips, news, giveaways and much more!

YoungWritersUK   YoungWritersCW   youngwriterscw

SCAN ME TO WATCH THE POETRY SAFARI VIDEO!